AF889441

THE HALO RULE

Copyright © 2008 by Teresa Leo. All rights reserved.

Author Photo: Jason Eskenazi

Cover Art: *Virtue #8*, by Judith Schaechter,
Stained glass, 34" x 31", 2003.

Book Design: Joel A. Bass

ISBN: 1-932418-25-3

Elixir Press
PO Box 27029
Denver, Colorado 80227

www.ElixirPress.com

Elixir Press is a nonprofit literary organization.

6-15-08
NYC

THE HALO RULE

For Jason + Michael —
Fellow poets + fabulous hosts —
Thanks for the great barbecue in
Bed-Stuy! Hope ~~to~~ see you both
again soon!
All the best,
Teresa

Teresa Leo

Teresa Leo

ELIXIR PRESS

Acknowledgments

My gratitude to the Pew Fellowships in the Arts, the Leeway Foundation, and the Pennsylvania Council on the Arts for fellowships or grants; to the Virginia Center for the Creative Arts, the Blue Mountain Center, and the Vermont Studio Center for residencies; and to the editors of the following publications in which versions of these poems have appeared:

The American Poetry Review: "Narcissists Anonymous," "To the Next in Line"

The American Poetry Review's Philly Edition: "Aubade," "Can't," "Don't"

Barrow Street: "The Double Ds of Desire and Despair"

Italian Americana: "First Kiss"

La Petite Zine: "Given," "Leavings," "Saturn"

New Orleans Review: "Chance Encounter"

Painted Bride Quarterly: "Junkie," "The Lasting"

The Philadelphia Inquirer: "Love at the End of the 20th Century," "No Atheists"

Ploughshares: "Yes But"

Poetry: "The World According to Narcissus"

The Portable Boog Reader Philadelphia: "Move"

Women's Review of Books: "P.S.," "Song of Woo with a Hole in It"

Xconnect: "Either Side of the Mason-Dixon," "Lingual," "The One Narcissus Almost Loved," "Storm Door," "Unsayable," "Vanishing Point," "The Visit"

"Anniversary" was published in *Mooring Against the Tide: Writing Fiction and Poetry* (Prentice Hall, 2005).

"Call Across the Seasons" and "P.S." appeared on the Waywiser Press web site as work samples from semi-finalists/finalists for the 2006 Anthony Hecht Poetry Prize.

"No Atheists" was reprinted in *Owner Operator.*

"The World According to Narcissus" appeared on *Poetry Daily.*

My deepest thanks to my family, especially my parents, Robert and Anna Mae Leo, and to the following people who have had an impact on my life and work: Robin Becker, Stephen Berg, David "Lefty" Bonanno, Lisa Borders, Fran Campo, Christopher Chambers, Kateri Chambers, Dana Curtis, David Deifer, Linh Dinh, Michael Duffy, Stephen Dunn, Annette Earling, Jason Eskenazi, Kevin Ferris, David Floyd, Sarah Hannah, my friends and colleagues at Information Systems & Computing at Penn, Marcella Kaczmarcik, Patrick Kelly, everyone at Kelly Writers House, Jeff Knorr, Yusef Komunyakaa, John Mulhern III, Miriam Olson, Toby Olson, Karl Patten, Jeffrey Plunkett, Elizabeth Scanlon, Kathleen Sheeder, Maurya Simon, Bruce Smith, Susan Stewart, John Timpane, Kathleen Volk Miller, Marion Wrenn, and most especially, Deirdre O'Connor and Jack Wheatcroft.

THE HALO RULE

I.

II.

III.

IV.

For Deirdre O'Connor

The halo rule is the two-yard circle of life given to punt returners. Any defender who encroaches upon that circle is guilty of interference. The idea is to protect the returner, who is looking up in order to catch the ball and can't protect himself from the hit of a defender running full speed with mayhem on his agenda.

—Ivan Maisel, *Sports Illustrated*

I would hope you, too,
would hold something back,

and that you'd always want
whatever unequal share
you had style enough to get.

—Stephen Dunn

I.

P.S.

The end is not near. We've passed the end, and it's so far back
it's like the tit of a cow in a field of poppies, a dot in a field

of many dots in a painting a myopic man is straining to see
in a village museum near a city we've never been to

nor will. It's so far back I can't remember the exact
moment of it, the way I didn't see the curve ball coming,

the one that clipped my left hip as I swung the bat,
missing and not being missed. It's the part of the eraser

worn down to the black metal band, the one that left
hideous gashes in the page of the test the math teacher

sprung on us, so many equations without solutions,
numbers that divided like soldiers on a reconnaissance mission,

then divided again. It's in the back of the closet
in the box of Thank You cards I put stamps on

and never sent. It's that last conversation,
the staccato of conjunctions that kept each noun at bay,

the one that wound down to the luxury of nonspecifics—
the possibility of *or,* the horror of *but,* the delusion of *and.*

It passed me by, the way beauty, like disease,
has been known to skip a generation.

Suite for the Possessed

Let's say we didn't, tragically, in the elevator
at the airport Hilton, between floors, the numbers

stacked like a poker hand seen but not raised.
The kiss, if not gasoline, then turpentine,

or two red peonies in a cardboard tube
with the poster, its hidden message, the moon's

"bald eye staring back through the drapes."
We're two mouths bruised by the ordinary,

the equal but opposite torque and rotation,
artifacts of nightshade, phone calls, time zones,

of concrete and voices we hear in our heads.
I won't say I'm fire and in it, that his stark white vest

conjured old world royalty, an earl
sent to make peace with a rival country.

When the doors open at 16, he pulls back *(mal occhio)*,
the bright heart a passage *(jettatura)*,

then dread. I know the lateral and play it, that hand:
first felony, last flight, no fold, this floor.

Lingual

I talk in my sleep, right brain only,
apparently and without logic,

out loud and context-free. Two words:
diffusion, agitation, then the body forks

and triangulates to rhythms that start at the back
of the throat. A Hebrew letter is trying to escape,

and I read like a *sadhe* or maybe a *heth,*
a visual scat that keeps him up to see what's next:

a collapse of empires, implosion of buildings,
earthquake, fire riot, car chase, dogs,

Sarajevo under siege. He closes in then,
folds between synapse and seizure

to squeeze out the narration but not the story:
dilapidate, diminish, diffusion, ruin.

And this becomes another story
that will end, eventually, in letters and limbs,

the ascenders and descenders of bodies
that snap together lyrically at night.

But it's the story after that, the one that bolts
in the not-quite-hysteric, not-quite-visceral blink

of morning that we will believe,
that book of hours that wraps fingers

and tongues around hard edges,
where his hand on the small of my back

is a stone tablet carved
from the heft and muscle of trouble and sleep.

The Double Ds of Desire and Despair

are in the long, slow torso of a woman bent back, seeing
and not being seen. It's a cache problem: a steady line

of two-faced two-fers on a Saturday night, the Double Divas
porn site he logged off of when she walked in the room.

No honesty counter, no small-breasted action figure
to save this boy who meets the world

then checks his e-mail before he shuts down.
He spins around in his chair with the kind of satisfaction

that comes from the gotten-over-on,
the something-well-transacted, the just-got-greased.

This is the old fish story that legends are made of,
not the come-heres and fisticuffs of what actually happened,

what made her go to the living room,
let him finger her while watching the movie,

the way he'll be distracted, later, during sex,
by Rodin's *Nude* hanging over the bed

like a broad-band vision of all that looks good
but doesn't speak. When he starts the NC-17 talk

in her ear, she listens carefully, arches her back,
murderous and sentimental, like a staircase.

Storm Door

The first time I ran through glass
was nothing compared with tonight's slaughter:

goblet, martini, highball, shooter—all cast
from the same family of complex triggers

and outright grief. A five-letter word that means
"can shatter," with a jigger of scotch

that's two fingers shy of what he needs,
now, to take the edge off,

to not vault across the table
and play Rock-Paper-Scissors on the back

of my head. He throws drinks at the wall
the way Ali threw punches, hard, without warning,

roped dopes and blinding jabs.
With us, it's always more rock than paper,

under the influence of too much daylight,
the way a screen door, left open,

is indistinguishable from its see-through cousin,
closed, an optical illusion of downstairs basement

just past glass. Precise entry means less scarring,
more paper, a cinderblock with wings,

the way what's swallowed whole can go down smoothly,
unknifelike, double-malted, three fingers, uncocked.

Pine Barrens

Chokehold. First the swerve, the only way
to cross three lanes of highway,

cut and groove through New Jersey
badlands, steering wheel, fingerprints,

a silver Mexican Morse Code necklace,
dots and dashes around the throat

just south of the jaw line.
The usual routine. If you saw us, later,

at the restaurant, we'd look hopeful,
the it that it can only be when it's not

thinking. Not blameful, more
airless, arcless, the gist of the story:

a curled thing, the way a kiss becomes
a means to an end, a crack, a window,

a collarbone. A pleasant ride home.
The restorative properties of darkness.

Saturn

after Goya

Last night I drank the coffeetable—
twenty dollars here, an armchair there,

soon I'll be eating whole dressers, credenzas,
arms and legs like limbs that dangled
over the bed in a memory of naked bodies,

anything I can get my hands on,
anything we brought together
to make this place *our* place;

I'll consume the house.

Engagement Sonnet

He takes back the ring. Out of bounds but not
off limits, not unlike childhood, the wiffle ball
sometimes stuck in the tree. In bed, after martinis,
the fight that escalated from fingernails to headboard,
left hook, bodyslam, peeled plaster, half-cocked:
he's no squire on bent knee with a jewel lodged
in a velvet pillow. He's half made, half unmade,
a man in bed, propped on one arm, face of a boy
who chips it high and takes off without looking
to see where it goes. I've played the field enough
to know what follows a pitch that breaks
when it crosses the plate. A high swing. Some wind.
A batter on deck and one in the hole. *Do over,* he says,
this ain't the big leagues, no foul, no keeps.

Chance Encounter

Not an intersection at noon in the heat of summer.
More a dark alley abandoned at midnight
or an organ transplant with scissors, the line

of a shoulder slumped against concrete
as we approach each other out on the street.
He thinks he's Eightball Comics and Bazooka Joe,

passion without perdition, the hair on his head
four shades blonder than that on his chin.
This man, who stood outside a fetishes boutique

wanting what turns men into women and women
into shadows, came back between legs, between seizures,
smelling like an animal migrating the tundra,

until something like turpentine rose and then caught
at the back of his throat. Now, nowhere to run,
the way he did it, last time, away from the apartment,

no words, no gestures, nothing like *welcome*
or *never again*. When that moment comes on the sidewalk,
we're random, stiff as cornstalks, surrounded by shingling

in a city where even the serial killers have wives,
and can't stop, late, or very early in the morning,
when he will disappear again roughly, and again.

The Visit

He sits there, oblivious. What if I said
G-string, tantric, curvature, spine.

Ninety-nine percent ready to bolt, the next flight,
Birmingham, leave this hundred degree

tundra of charbroiled drawls
and curtains that float. The *Sturm und Drang*

of it, tapdance, but not suspect. If I could run,
I'd fly: America does not start

here. Two couches beside but not equal to,
the obscene rhetoric of exposure

and ash. What next, the paper or telephone,
transported to time zones not

in this room. We're flatlined, sandblasted,
pummeled, untoward. The effacement exercise

goes something like this:
scintiscan, watershed, pivot, farce.

A pastiche, not parody, at least not
when *disclosure* is three or four pages

west of *desire*. He must sense this,
turning to look. There's something to say.

Vanishing Point

Idiot. What I said 7 or 8 times in the bathroom after.
After sex, after the confession that came out

like clockwork, two months in,
two mouths on one head, too soon to say it,

but the *beaujolais village,* something light in August,
and no pause, no clutch, no drive train coupling,

just me and Best of The Doobies
spinning in the dark. Love.

He wants to smoke. Naked, nothing, no preamble,
it's dark, it's da Vinci on screen-saver,

living room computer, the idiot moment
under the skin. Da Vinci, backlit,

panels that bounce, all orthogonals and line drawings,
the stuff that aerodynamics and corners are made of.

He wants to cook. Penne or angel hair,
white or red, asparagus or projectiles that veer off,

take shape into objects that fly. This doesn't.
He wants patience, pause, but I can't say

and study the screen: a synecdoche that isn't,
two panels cross and are lost.

One enters and the other exits: da Vinci is
grinder/papermill/printer, wings-on-hinge, gadgets,

parts that come full circle and stop. We're paralyzed,
sfumato, magnetized to forks and can't look up.

Long train running, *not,* the parmesan draglined
all to one side. He wants to know if it'll be weird.

The *beaujolais's* gone and now beer, Jamaican,
something with tang, as if only the foreign could stand

for what's vacating, visceral, seizing, shocked.
Not weird, but lateral, where *across* means

bypass, sidestep, around-the-bend, through.
I know the pitch and scale, the *someday* and *maybe then,*

the look of the room when it's starting to shrink.
We're going there, fully, airborne and without caveat,

all barrel springs, curvature, gradations of shadows
landing on spheres. I can't make it stop.

Sisyphus in Reverse

To see them
        sitting on the park bench

with their heads thrown back,
        looking up at tree branches

against the fall sky,
        her head tucked

in the dark nook
        of his arm,

his head tilted
        to almost meet hers

at the crown,
        scanning for a leaf

to loosen and spin
        its simple chaos to the ground,

you'd think they were in love.
        They were not.

The leaves stayed put,
        accomplished everything.

II.

The Halo Rule

intends to protect
a return man by two yards.
Even in football

the defenseless man
has an unimpeded chance
for a fair catch if

he waves his arm while
the kick is in flight. Not so
elsewhere. For us, it's

sideswipe, no berth, the
deference of play to hurt,
rough lust. For us, there's

no homosocial
verve, no return man. Our most
grievous infractions.

Narcissists Anonymous

A jackal among hedgehogs. At the meeting,
N. looked around, not sure why him,

why he was forced to occupy a room
with these almost-but-not-quite paragons

of beauty, all magnificently groomed,
but whacked in a way he knew he was not.

And N. knew their grooming was the artifice
of grooming, the way some animals lick their paws clean

after stepping in shit. But they visually appealed
and he didn't mind looking at them,

one in particular, the more-and-better
of her elongated neck, the kind men sculpt statues

to immortalize, in the row before him.
When her neck moved, the woman's shirt moved,

lifted to show the black line of a G-string
and the tip of an angel tattoo. N. liked the way

the wing's veins etched low on the woman's hip,
the dark lines that arced in and out of view.

He liked imagining the tattoo's complexity,
the pain it must have caused her,

and began thinking of ways he'd follow the neck,
from curve to hip, cast the angel earthward

before the night was through. Then, N. got distracted
by the pristine condition of his own hands,

the length and width of his delicate fingers.
He thought of how the woman

would notice his hands first, the way all women did,
and how she'd be unable to stop herself

from thinking about what those fingers
would feel like inside her, which would force her

to shift in her seat, which would raise her shirt,
expose the G-string, and play in N.'s mind

like the opening of a sonata, which in turn would
thunderbolt down his torso to the backs of his knees,

and, for a second, feel something like shame.
It passed. The meeting broke. The woman

stood and turned. He was already thinking
of the beautiful and various ways he could leave her.

The World According to Narcissus

Her. But not her. Her. N.'s whole world
was broken down like this,

into the women he would or would not
have. With some, it was whether

they had the kind of beauty
that cauterized eyes, the one hundred fictions

of it, like chokeweed that could root
anywhere and begin to thrive.

With others, he measured potential,
their ability to slip from contemporary cotton

into cocktail shooters, a brown sugar backstory
that could start, say, in a cornfield,

aroused by a little subjugation, verbs
he'd take a shine to when he'd single her out:

lure, charm, exhaust, burn. Either way
it had to turn. In the beginning, peonies.

Eventually, gasoline. When it did turn,
he'd weigh the *baroque/throat*

rhyme of her beauty against everything legal,
find ways to unbecome it, an elegance

he'd chip away at and have, and not have, and have
until it was a broken thing, a bird unwinged.

Until she was a ghost.
He did not have an eye for ghosts.

Narcissus and the Charm Motel

Three hours of dirt and diesel
to meet a small town girl

at The Blue Daze Lounge,
three hours N. would eventually

have to asphyxiate out of her,
for her own good, to unharm her,

say, eight months later
at the Charm Motel,

the place where he would take them
when he was ready to flee.

A buzz saw. Phantoms.
An uppercut followed by a one-two punch

that she wouldn't see coming
when her time was up, say,

on July 19, 1997, with or without mercy,
with or without smokes,

those early morning sequences
of disjointed hallucinations

and haunting dreams.
N. was more serial than linear,

like all men she loved,
but she waited for him

a long time anyway,
searched under the heavy neon

of other motels up and down
the interstate, anywhere felonies

were committed with regularity or style.
Back at the Charm, she noticed, finally,

the C had lost its hold, burned out.
The difference between *charm* and *harm*

was never more than a read/delete
slip of the tongue, a letter, a screw.

The One Narcissus Almost Loved

he wooed relentlessly through every possible media
(e-mail, U.S. Mail, phone, fax, UPS, and FedEx),

and, in a fit of Baudelaire-induced hallucinations,
said he'd never leave her on a fifteen mile run

in the middle of a cornfield; the one whose hair
he said induced a deep, cortextual howl,

the one who came to believe it and said
she loved him while sitting in the V

of his legs facing the spigot in the bathtub
of a roadside motel in New Hampshire,

after which she said, "And you?"
to which N. replied that he was not

all the way there yet,
which made her think of Neruda's lines

"I love my own lost self, my faulty stuff,
my silver wound and my eternal loss,"

while she studied the geometric patterns
on the bathroom wallpaper,

hoping to see in it an apparition
or at least the face of the Virgin,

something to distract her
from committing a felony of some kind—

the one N. almost loved
slowly became an echo,

a voice, a sluicing
water in red dust and coal,

the nape of a neck not quite albatross,
not quite clay; an outline, a trace.

Anniversary

I said I wouldn't, the date that started on the back stairs,
birdfeeder empty because November meant silence
or bodies stiff from the freeze, the blue-black mouths

that choked back breath in the wind.
I don't need to go there, the juke joint, the pool cue
and speech impediment, your reckless car, a lent heart

joyriding the cornfields, and me, bright lights,
small-town girl with a decent shot from the top of the key,
all rural routes and vegetable stands, a duck pond in winter

with a vague, imperceptible longing, spring rain.
We drove the cow country, bags of peat moss we stole
wedged in the trunk, two 8-balls, felons, delirious

from the bereft/theft rhyme of *desire* and *seizure*
under our skin. Now that you've called to remind me,
to hear it break in your voice like a bank shot,

the three years blow open again, jumping betties,
booby traps, and it's 6 a.m. with the engine on,
windowfog, your hand on my finger

pressed against the glass, our secret chirography:
cellar door. You ask how I am. I'm dazed, damaged,
living too long under a stark coal miners' sky.

I block the shuck and jive, the *take me, shake me*
of Solomon Burke, the concrete and talk, torso,
tangle of birds on electric wires, one always opposite

the rest before it suicides and takes off.
But I say *good* and you say *great,* then we disconnect,
two fugitives, and disappear again

into the cruel complicity of self-imposed exile,
knowing that no matter what safehouse,
what asylum of state lines and time zones,
there is no witness protection for the lost.

Move

Coming fast like a jail on wheels. Up I-95
through Wilmington, past the airport exit

and concrete meridian, an aerialist maneuver
over asphalt, his move. How, if at all,

does narrative fit in, the double-clutch
of *vacate or ready the pacemaker,*

brake or blow up, somewhere between hometown
and exile, grace and militia, this chase, then choke,

then deadened again. How, if at all,
does adjacency fit in, the militant but not mindful,

his four: *lust, luster, lash, then less and less.*
Not encounters over 8-Ball, oblivion over gumbo,

more a nuclear warhead buried in the backyard,
an all-points bulletin, the neighborhood and sex offense,

the platonic, what's banned. How, if at all,
does agency fit in, the morose but not mutable,

my four: *drugged, deranged, demonized, damaged.*
Not speculum before lap dance, head cleaner

before hanging, more a bloodletting contest
anonymous without mirrors, the forehead and collarbone,

surrendered but not emphasized, a six-month frenzy,
italic and uncensored, what's blown, just blown.

Acknowledgments

Not a word, a mention, a nomenclature or coda.
No wedding rings, cock rings, nothing animal,
arcane, or otherwise brutal. Just a book of poems

in a stark white envelope, little disclosures
that sway into oblivion the way bamboo floor boards
give suddenly under the body, its weight.

But the inscription, black ink on the title page:
"W/ Love." I've heard better, the innocuous ways
men sign off, disappear in pixels to remote corners

of banana bush, peony, counterfeit slogans
that hide desire, the way an outhouse
in a buffalo field of a rural village

has wood slats for standing, tries to mask
the unmaskable, good catch: *Regards, take care, best,*
be well, sincerely, later, and (occasionally) *with affection.*

Don't think I don't know the book of hours:
I've seen them click past the way short women
in high heels stoop and splinter under the pretense,

the precision of what they are called upon
to endure. Not now, not ever, he said,
offending the universe against the familiar

of clouds and stars. I think of distance
as famine/feminine, not "more and better later,"
the alternate ending of who's last standing,

who disappoints best, with the greatest intent.
The felonious turned formalist, it's
how to abide what he is called upon to say.

Googling Him:
The One Whose Name Must Not be Spoken is

not racing for victory at Indianapolis
still a force
a Regent's Professor of Economics
a native of El Reno
very familiar with the community college environment
a republic supporter
getting up there in age
himself a complex man with artwork that invites viewers
        into the complexity
one of the most original
the author of three books of poetry
a professional you can trust by viewing the member profile
setting up the game for one more power play
the author of four books of poetry
still in the game
whining now
an a cappella aficionado
still a force
listed as questionable with a strained shoulder
        and not able to practice
president and CEO
still around
a very unethical and inept attorney
39 years old
serving at San Quentin
senior vice president of commercial property
arrogant as well as clueless
credited on certain CDs
looking for Thinkers past whom to run some "notions"
the all-time master of the genre
a modern painter of religious scenes
the latest addition
not bad either
like the Regis Philbin of travel
the undisputed national pruning champion
an amazing player

designing a system to prevent this from happening
expected to introduce something that would regulate
        nighttime lighting in Pennsylvania
definitely showing his age
adroit in his use of animation
still effective
the ringleader
the supervising animator
a player who must be accounted for
most likely gone
still powering his heavy freight up the mountain

Call Across the Seasons

Four Octobers ago, upstairs at the Halloween party,
prone on the bed. Still in the post mortem

of the last phone call, where the definition of *abide*
meant more *putting up with* than *being there for,*

as in, disappointment, as in, an obscene bouquet
of something seasonal next to the bed,

the bed's coiling crushed beneath my collapsed,
my vacant body, a seizure in reverse.

Downstairs the party went on,
a gross disproportion of forgiveness and light.

I didn't know then that four years later
the next call would come,

the way wind can go from zero to a hundred
in 2.5 seconds, tear the trees from the trees,

as in, a door flung open, as in, lovers at a party
looking for an empty room, coats sprawled on beds,

like the long dead or newly rehearsed.
He'd say my name wrong after just four years,

would want to know what became of the peony
pressed in the pages of a book,

that flawed dance. But he'd really mean
fire, as in, there's no way to fully escape

the tyranny of certain flowers,
the ones that fail overnight or flame

between the pages of a long lost book.
What would matter in the end

is that he'd say my name wrong,
say it outright without hesitation,

a perverted overture, this law of eternal return,
ghost bed, a deep-six version, a strangled vowel.

Song of Woo with a Hole in It

When you leave,
take the embalmed summer squash

you sent through the mail
as a sign of affection,

the apricot pit
you sucked to the bone

then thrust in my mouth
during the first kiss

of our first night of bedpost
and fruit and nylon seduction;

take the choice Adorno quotes
you used to explain

the half-hearted handholding
at the river in that New England city

where you snuffed out
every possible chance

for me to say it out loud;
take the poolhall serenade,

the see-and-raise metaphors,
the mouth and neck allusions,

the overtold stories
of wrists and teeth.

Despite the Elizabethans,
I do not love you

or your adjectives;
so take all those bandaged moments,

the ruined voice, the dark space
between tooth and lip I'll miss.

III.

To the Next in Line

Don't think he means it, the dash that's vague
between letters and you. He's said it before:

out loud, in half-light, a waif and stutter,
this busted shoe beyond repair, closed fist,

hangnail that grows backward into the skin.
You'll want to believe. You'll want to stop

wanting the packages that befuddle the U.S. Post:
pressed violets, summer squash, maple leaf,

vial of sandalwood, that stray piece of polished glass.
Whatever you think, there were, literally, a hundred

before you. The not quite dead and the nearly lost,
all shank and muscle for the days to come.

Just once, during sex, look over your shoulder to see
the not-quite-there of the not-quite-thereness behind you.

He will, of course, be looking away, will push
your head back to the bed so you can't see him

not seeing you: "I see you and raise you.
I promise no bruise. Come find me at night

and we'll go up in flames." You will remember
everything about wrists, the way they'll crawl

on their own to the hip and ache.
Seedling, flower power, stress, repressed dream.

This is the map without the territory.
This is a voice with a missing J.

Thumb under eye, two fingers under chin,
the Campo de' Fiore, nerves that end

with a German twang. It's bitten by salt
and not without sweetness, that film noir:

the day is a wing ripped off a starling.
Talk is a saltlick and some smoke.

Touch is grounds for what he's doing
when he's doing you.

In Bed, After

Skin smooth as winter
they watch rain arming shadows
beneath love   a knife

Poets in Particular

Nights when narrative wraps thighs
and drops bodies to the floor,
we don't need adjectives

to describe the sharps and flats of a voice
or limbs dangling like gerunds
in a moment of syntax broken in the light

Verbs handle participles as delicately
as he rises and falls to the rhythm of
the can't, the don't, the yes but, the not

The penis a question marking the spot
where legs split like infinitives
ready to tear the lids off syllables

No diphthong strong as two minds
that take their conjuncting seriously:
but not, or this, and then

qualifiers—

The room full of particulars

Words lost in their origins

No apostrophes here

Can't

After we fuck, he comes to himself,
back from a scattering of parts and phrases,

pulled from a starkness too violent to remember
(though fragments jostle in back of the eyes

in a furious attempt to make it)
and says: "I can't *do* more than this."

Despite the impression of skin in skin, bodies
orbiting the sofa from some place more primitive

than this, crumbs swept neatly from the table
or stones, he steps back to himself in stages:

shoes last, the sofa, talk of hardware stores
and shrink wrap, how cold it's been for a month

like this, the door. To walk the streets
with the certainty of sex, sure as sound and space

have no choice but to slam up against each other
like the back of a hand turned quickly to the face

or some snatch of conversation that meant so much
you can't remember where you heard it or when,

he comes to himself, fully now, and, with the grace
of a forgotten birthday, starts one remarkable arm

across the sofa, fingers gone limp as small men
who've carried something too far

and can't find a place for it,
quick, short breaths to remember;

they come between us like nothing,
like air.

Don't

tell me I'm beautiful or I have a perfect body
or that we could move in 4/4 time
to a house across the street from my best friend,
someone you think I could drink coffee with

late mornings when you're still not home,
when the sun takes over the sky
like the bloated and graceless thing it was
and would be. It won't work,

that stupid grin I fell for once,
even the skin under the left ear
won't draw my tongue, like your tongue on me,
crazy and determined to transport me somewhere

you think I can't get to without you.
The way you listen now, carefully,
as though I were describing the exact moment
of your death (no doubt by fire)

doesn't con me: even if the penis,
the demon that it is, could hard bop
in double-time like Sonny Stitt's tenor sax
in "There Are Such Things,"

I wouldn't have you,
you, who brought the *I Ching*
and tarot readers to divine ecstasy
over my whole life (first fire then water)

but it's too late; I'm done.
You're a speck of light on the shirt
of an ordinary man on the street.
Not Dizengoff, not Tel Aviv,

not that beach during the thunderstorm
where you said my hair was a creature
unto itself, a dark and dangerous thing
that could set the world on fire.

Yes But

The stance of desire. At the garden party,
her face toward his mouth and he points
and calls them by name: peony, rhododendron,
foxglove, their finger-shaped corollas,

the cardiac stimulant of digits that lead
to a woman's heart. From the footbridge,
I watch him and his other lover
poke fingers into the mouths of open flowers.

Those Chinese finger traps that stick,
like the imprint of thumbs on skin,
the way he'll do it, later,
above the suprasternal notch,

because this is before concrete and metal
in distant rain, lines before gestures,
before the double-block of *no harm, no foul,*
the *yes but* of wrists burning against velvet,

the two-finger chord he'll play on the throat,
and lipstick a shade too dark,
the sound of his voice when he'll say *don't.*
But now, dusk. Bats drop from the sky

like gestures of good faith. We're alone
when he pulls me under the clothesline,
takes my wrist and tells me
it's safe. I memorize the soft lines of his face

until the flowers fade, the footbridge,
and forgive him for what will become
the lovetaps and suckerpunch of morning,
when I'll have to shake out the numbness

but not the fire, felon, arranged heart, brooding
flower that splits the concrete, even when he leaves,
even when disease becomes the last form
of self-expression, the hip, the lip, the distance

nothing more than a torch song.
But tonight the lines run over my head.
They loop back on themselves, a warning,
this but no further, as if a resonance is here

with no hope of there being anything more,
as if only the bats could fall crazy to earth and return.

Not (Another Love Poem)

Figliomini is dead. And Nonny, hooked up
to that wheeze-eazy she yanked from her nostrils
to say what my mother wouldn't translate

from Napoletano. It was Friday.
Still thinking about screens for my windows
and Figliomini's Drugs back on Fallbrook.

Vague memories of Nonny bantering
over the counter in a language that shook
my body and slipped off a small mind

distracted by jars of Twizzlers.
Now her thick fingers pulling me
down to my knees:

"za boyfriendina, e's a comina?"
How to translate, in so many words,
the sheer numbness of watching

a taxi cab burn on a busy street,
lights I saw in the basement
when my mother told me: "he's dead."

Still not married, not one green avocado
in the refrigerator, no one like my brother
left to hold on to in the dank cubicle

of a neighbor's basement. Those children
were mean. If not for my brother's sobbing,
that garden hose on full blast every 5 minutes

like something to depend on—
I thought I'd die at 7
doing loop de loops from the driveway

up to the tree on the corner. The love
of a yellow banana seat bike,
but in the circling, our family's life story cut from

and leading to a village outside of Naples,
I knew, in so many words,
the peasant dresses I wore stood for something.

Something most probably green.
And if green was the color of childhood,
the color of unlocked doors and draglines,

where nights in backseat alleys with strip mine boys
meant language stripped down
to underwear with someone else's boyfriend,

then not Figliomini, not this man's roving eye
or brightness, not the solitude
of another pair of shoes left at the bed

like someone walked out and kept going.
More a body, a face, each muscle out of whack,
certain the next syllable will be utterly gelatinous,

whole sides of sentences unbalanced,
the teeth gone numb as nails.
More the words and never enough.

Bellissimo

Never exactly an insider, but strong:
a coal miner's wife, an immigrant, an arranged marriage.

Nonny, *sentinella* of the house, the family, watching over,
dusting the hand-painted plaster statues on the credenza,

her forfeited world: olive trees, the Old Country,
the Neapolitan memory of a language brought to her tongue

and lost. Her inherited world: the color of slag at midnight,
the curve of a man's back from too much drink,

a vocabulary of words suspended like figs, just out of reach.
Beauty in the act of dusting the statues of saints against a backdrop

of breakers and draglines. Beauty in the hook of the back
from bending, the bread dough and sauce on her dress,

the tissues stuffed in the apron pockets. Beauty in the gift
of what's let go, the opposite of exile, that other life.

First Kiss

Viaduct, overpass, backwood, breaker.
It was '76 in coal country, dragline and mine fire,

a bicentennial that wasn't for our town,
between the projects and Orchard Street,

at 13, the terrible knocking of teeth.
It was Sicily against Naples,

shrines and the Old Country,
sentinel against lawn Virgin,

nothing but lips and grapes at the breast,
skin in the bushes of the East Side graveyard.

It was Tony Tolerico—
roughneck, bad boy, gearhead,

a breaking and entering between the headstones
of Bruno and Angelini that morphed:

the great stone face of my father
waiting for me to mow the lawn,

his hands, rusted grip, the mower,
yanking the pull cord, idle, engine, off.

But the mouth of Saint Anthony,
portable and without grace.

Anthony, hammer, finder of things,
or the other one,

guardian of butchers and gravediggers.
He could say *stay* and *always* in two languages,

a corrupt tongue and a body I believed.
Later in the driveway, my father looked up

from his truck for a moment, and, without speaking,
disappeared again under the hood.

Disappeared the way the thick, foreign names
of our grandparents attracted the soles of our shoes

then let us slip off, disappeared like a trail
of fresh-cut grass away from our houses

and the lives we'd leave there.
And Tony, in 8th grade, with a blonde girl

from another school. The overlapping circles,
outlined by tiny ridges of dark green,

a layer of skin pulled back like an altered memory:
my father, watching from the porch,

the smell of fresh-cut grass
the only thing I found that mattered.

Junkie

I'm an off-ramp, a throughway, the last exit
        on the Pennsylvania Turnpike,

where the cashier said I look like a cross
        between Elaine from *Seinfeld*

and Alanis Morissette, or his high school prom date,
        who he left to get high with a cheerleader,

bleachers, blackout, a second down
        at the last home football game of the season.

It's late fall and I'm at it again,
        this infrared night scope heart,

a heat-seeking missile
        when desire sets in over 8-Ball,

three games at the pool hall on Delaware Ave.
        His Jagermeister to my Yuengling,

it's the stop-and-go between strokes, radar
        between bank shots, then the pull-back caveat

of *I like you but.* He wants to go.
        How can I say it's not me, really,

a sex addict, a two-pack-a-day freestyle junkie.
        I like you too, but too late, stoplight,

and it's the pitch-and-hurl, the drop-and-roll,
        and he's out of the car and gone.

In my apartment, it's cow country,
        the summer of '77, those four-corners

where I slung softees at the Tastee Freeze.
        At 14, out back dumping mop water,

I was nothing, nothing but jailbait
in a polyester jumpsuit,

hand-crushed chocolate on a soft cone stick.
The boy who thought he was Superman,

who wanted coffee without kryptonite,
waited out back by the dumpster,

said *come here* and *do this.*
Under the hijack sky

and neon of 52 flavors of shake,
I unzipped: the reckless display

of skin and skin. I knew then
it would be like this, always,

something anonymous, something airborne,
an unfinished building in an urban nightscape,

where, years later, if I could get away with it,
I'd jackknife from the 13th floor

and go back to cornfields,
to a stoplight at a four-corners

cycling through its harsh, conventional logic—
go, then don't go, then go.

The 20-Spot

What came after was not backlash or bliss.
It was off Route 6, the gravel road

to the 0-6 Rod and Gun Club,
in the brush where the creek

to the fish hatchery met the tree line,
at 16, the nerve, the note and end note

of wild mushrooms and swallows,
reed worms and crab thistle,

that place where accidents happen,
we lay. Nothing, not the exhaust,

not the killdeer watering up
before their fall excursions

away from this place of noun and verb
and deep redemption could stop us.

Who knew it meant nothing to him then
as it still would not, 20 years later,

when we'd lie together again on the flatbed
of a pickup off RR 2, a pull-off

on the one-laner toward Elk Mountain,
variations on a theme:

one hand down, a mouth,
a reunion of the 13 ways to distraction

among the paint buckets and concrete
of his inground pool business,

rapture, enrapture, ungraceful, that thrill.
To know the shame and to do it anyway

is a bloodshot, broken, 3 a.m. kind of knowing
where the chamber of brainmass splits

from the skull, a friction of class and aesthetics,
the place where the lovesick hear voices,

get burnt. He was the one who taught me
to unlove and unhear the voices,

to dull the thump of possibility
and heat—the unsadness of two bodies

tangled around leaf skimmers
undoing each other all night.

IV.

Leavings

As if rearranging things on the restaurant table
could speak of what's slipped between us:
the glass moved to the center,
water that takes the shape and holds it

the way the city on a clear night holds the sky.
A suspended distraction of lights
too numerous to count. If I can't
hold on to the glass or stand still

at the bathroom door without shaking,
the sound of the lock snaps my frame
and brings me back to the ordinary ritual
of leaving. How the woman departs

and looks over her shoulder, a look that says
it's all yours now, the little things that matter:
hair in the sink, the outline her lips leave on paper,
the little good-byes. Her lips are

too bold a color for a day that gathers itself
into one recoverable moment of loss,
the way tables turn over and people
take to the room for a while,

give context to the memory of him
fingering the tableware after he's gone.
Nothing like chairs to speak of people
coming and going like little leaps of faith.

New Year

Skiing in July,
fishing in February,

the days disjoint
and groove,

a meltdown of months,
a mind out of whack.

I'm still back at August
where the Beaujolais

that came
from 35 villages

fit sideways
inside my head,

the dorsal fin of it,
the brain slowed

por fin to belief.
Between then and now

the numbers,
an 8-Ball routine

jacked on polyethylene,
trees unmercifully diminished,

choked by maneuverings
and light.

I'll release last year
in May

when I shovel
the driveway

and go geologic,
a Paleolithic hell—

if each season
were twice as long

the year
would wear me well.

Either Side of the Mason-Dixon

Here, the shorty pool cue in the corner,
the one used for tight triangulations

when the edge of the doorframe blocks
a good bank shot, is a size 2-4 petite,

a Tasmanian devil in heels who watches boys
blow quarters and dividing lines

against a backdrop of nocturnes and shame.
There, where the bars close early or late,

the boys move body-wise around tables,
look for the line that the underage girls

will stretch their torsos to,
regardless of context or bearing.

Here, it's war-dress, urban shit-kickers
and black noir liner,

the scuttlebutt that wasn't on South Street,
no hound's-tooth or paisley or seersucker,

just pinprick, knifepoint, anatomy, vein.
There, in the land of the grit-fed,

big-busted women, a transcendental moment
is the confederate rock band's rendition

of "Sweet Home Alabama"
or Dixie's Blackened Voodoo Lager,

whichever goes down more smoothly
or first. Here, the sky is

sheet metal/brushed chrome/silver bullet/tin can,
whichever leaves a more suitable scar,

the day without you in it.
There, it's the aftermath of perpetuity, a rust color

that can't be painted over or rubbed out.
Here, *regardless* doesn't mean *without regard*

and the sun sets at a reasonable hour.
There, a wink is mere superstition

and the wind picks up regardless,
without warning, lashes the lean-tos

and shotgun shacks, and *harm* fulfills
all of its properties of grammar and rage.

Unsayable

for Leidy Sheeder Bonanno, 1981-2003

Here, it cannot end,
the place where I once
saw sparrows crosscut
raw, unblemished fields,
you who I did not
know, falling without
form, rage, the only
the most beautiful
word in the English
language, languish this:

what Paris, what place
we go but can't see,
what body adjusts
to non-light to tell
what's torn from what's here,
snow suffocates field,
you who I did not
know, the news, the one
story about what
happened, a twisted
spike in the gut of
our dark city I

don't want to believe,
it's like falling when
you who I did not
know but in some way
did, no words make sense,
it is without sense,
you, long hair pinned up,
more than a photo
on TV, lost worlds:
still, ache, mercy, fist,
a way of saying
not this, please, not this

Desiccant

They dare not speak.
Within them a line
not to be crossed,
a place that bears water,
contains. What cannot
be held spills off.
Across the room
a luxury of windows
too far gone,
a forgotten country,
the yellowed arm
of a neglected houseplant
angling beyond boundary;
they are a pair
with singular intent,
hers, grim parchment,
she writes them
as coda, dried flowers,
dark corners, two tongues.
Muteness, their territory.
Finished wrists
speak for themselves.

No Atheists

Thanks for the presence of mind
to cut the wheel before the brakes locked.

Driving 65 on 80 West, windows down,
air heavy with the smell of cow dung,

heat, then a bang, an explosion
with smoke but no fire.

Two tenths of me vacated my body,
rushed to a field where my ex-lovers

hunched in grief. I don't know why
the car cleared the lane

and stopped just short of the embankment,
what made me get out and stand like an animal

headlighted by my broken car. But thanks
for the truckers hauling propane to Cleveland,

Wendy and Mary Ann, the only ones
who stopped that hour I stood with the hood up,

pipelines and gaskets like organs exposed,
a body without skin. When that truck

pulled off the highway,
I ran toward it like the newly converted,

the grace of taillights red and blinking,
seizures in the dark.

Given

A day deliberate as a given in math:
the known is there for something to hold on to,
something that leafs through books and carries us
to answers about pi and the likelihood of decimals

repeating out of reach. It's like that,
a simple algorithm of four corners
coming together, the quadrangle of a dream,
where points leap out to powers higher

than the last argument made for the likes of it:
he read me poems. To know that dream,
how in it the sky turns a gray more impeccable
than what fingers dragged over a coffee table find—

if there were sines and cosines in grooves
of the furniture, a palpable distance of arcs
in wood thicker than what keeps him reading
beyond the end, I'd give over the things

that I've known: the sad geometry of people
gyrating in supermarkets, circumference of a desire
to stand firmly before cereal boxes
without crying. Crying over words

that leap off objects and insinuate themselves
into the context of our world.
To know the comfort of numbers and to accept
the impermanence of words, how figures transform

to shapes and colors, sheets lifted and snapped by wind,
how warm hands speak of objects
that touched us briefly: unshakable proof
of coming together and falling away on axes.

Love at the End of the 20th Century

I used to call it like this: stun gun, flame thrower,
harpoon, maimer. Whatever the charge,

the scarred heart followed; I loved like an army
at the brink of war—all battle plans, camouflage,

shoot-to-kill, seizures. The romance,
first tear gas, then morphine, nights

of white heat, sutures, slash-and-burn, shock.
But then, right at the end of the 20th century,

in the year of the hostage, as if dropped by chopper,
a bomb that didn't explode—you,

conscientious objector, accident, rapture,
and me, auto aim and rapid fire.

Then the words I'll carry to the other side changed:
mercy, surrender, standdown, light.

Though I'm no diplomat, no ambassador
of peace talks and treaties, I know the ricochet,

the arsenal, the ambushed heart.
I may be dangerous but I am not armed.

The Lasting

What we will remember is this—
in the graveyard late at night,
the brief curve of the body

as we hoisted ourselves up the cemetery wall,
that moment of hanging when weight shifted back
to some image of ourselves

holding out like kids in our parents' kitchens
when love fell away in knives and screams;
that moment when the ground took on the circumference

of lost connections: the inevitable walk
down childhood driveways, trophies we chalked up
outrunning ourselves, dreams of ourselves,

and the ground was hard. We scaled the wall
and lay down anyway, not like lovers,
but friends who knew the hysterical cry of mornings

when fear built in the belly and turned over
like a sweaty palm after a beating.
Stretched out on our backs,

you said the wind moved horizontally
through the trees. That you heard it move
across and not *down* the trees meant

you understood the vertical drop of too much
idle chatter, the way balance is everything recoverable,
the sky just a hunk of space for limbs to lock

and unlock at night. No amount of talk
could change the number of fortresses we built
just out of earshot of our parents' calling,

the black and blue houses we put our backs to,
each distinct step the first count of twenty paces
from everything we knew.

Mad Silhouette

Late at night,
when the light changes from blue to slate,

I hear from behind the wall
a brief, unshakable sound

like a small animal
brushing against wood.

I know the seasons behind that wall,
the reddish-brown tint of earth

packed like boxes of ex-lovers
moving from house to house,

the altitude where birds drift off
to secret wind tunnels and are lost.

If I pause to listen,
the sound stops in fits

and starts when I move—
naked, uncompromising,

this parry and counterpunch,
a syncopated tempo

of will and intent.
Shadows take to the room:

the estranged/deranged
call and response,

off-key, off-kilter,
an intersection of streets

where Wood meets Division,
Hope meets Power,

the mute improvisations
of a love-sick blood.

Aubade

Here, in this moment, street sweepers out
before first light breaks, branches heavy with ice,

I look for something stable in all this shifting:
the stray always outside, clanking through metal cans

as it forages for food. The hunting bear
turned in toward the house for a while,

satiated still by the body she raises toward him,
just so. To say *never* is to deny ice melting

onto clean streets, an entire night's sleep
when there's nothing to run away from in dreams.

To say *I'll never love you that way* is to see
in her face something heavy as olive trees,

something that tells of men turning to village
before last light falls;

I'll leave you someday tied to a fit of your own desires,
and our bodies will be wracked with pain.

That pain for free will, clad somewhat scantily
in a cool breeze, the shuddering

only an outward expression of the body internal.
Too much loss to believe in desert rain,

though I am told people have seen it,
coming fast over the hills. It's black

and powerful and cuts through sky,
the way blue eyes can go gray without warning.

The dead I've known have this in common:
at the end their eyes turned inward

as if they could see something,
cold as sidewalks, coming toward them.

Beyond that, the latch is off the gate again.
Everything homebound gets in.

Poetry Titles from Elixir Press

Circassian Girl by Michelle Mitchell-Foust
Imago Mundi by Michelle Mitchell-Foust
Distance From Birth by Tracy Philpot
Original White Animals by Tracy Philpot
Flow Blue by Sarah Kennedy
A Witch's Dictionary by Sarah Kennedy
Monster Zero by Jay Snodgrass
Drag by Duriel E. Harris
Running the Voodoo Down by Jim McGarrah
Assignation at Vanishing Point by Jane Satterfield
The Jewish Fake Book by Sima Rabinowitz
Recital by Samn Stockwell
Murder Ballads by Jake Adam York
Floating Girl (Angel of War) by Robert Randolph
Puritan Spectacle by Robert Strong
Keeping the Tigers Behind Us by Glenn J. Freeman
Bonneville by Jenny Mueller
Cities of Flesh and the Dead by Diann Blakely
The Halo Rule by Teresa Leo

Fiction Titles

How Things Break by Kerala Goodkin

Limited Edition Chapbooks

Juju by Judy Moffat
Grass by Sean Aden Lovelace
X-testaments by Karen Zealand
Rapture by Sarah Kennedy
Green Ink Wings by Sherre Myers
Orange Reminds You Of Listening by Kristin Abraham
In What I Have Done & What I Have Failed To Do by Joseph P. Wood
Hymn of Ash by George Looney
Bray by Paul Gibbons